It's Not Love, Unfortunately

A Selection of Relationship Poems

It's Not Love, Unfortunately

A Selection of Relationship Poems

Lylanne Musselman

Chatter House Press
Indianapolis, Indiana

It's Not Love, Unfortunately
A Selection of Relationship Poems

Copyright© 2018 by Lylanne Musselman

All rights reserved.

Except for brief quotations embodied in critical articles and reviews in newspapers, magazines, radio or television, no part of this book may be reproduced in any form or by any means electronic, mechanical, or by any information storage and retrieval system without written permission from the publisher.

For information:

Chatter House Press
7915 S Emerson Ave, Ste B303
Indianapolis, IN 46237

chatterhousepress.com

ISBN: 978-1-937793-50-0
Library of Congress Control Number: 2018949792

DEDICATION

This book is dedicated to Ann Johnson, for her encouragement and friendship, and for being a guiding force in my life since I was 15 years old. Her belief in me kept me going during times I certainly didn't believe in myself.

ACKNOWLEDGEMENTS

I would like to thank the editors of the journals and anthologies in which my poems originally appeared:

At Seventeen Series: Silver Birch Press – "Lasting Impressions"
Backlit Barbell: Kind of a Hurricane Press – "No Swimming"
Big Windows Review: WCC Press – "Driven," "Music Quitter," and "Weddings"
Brevity Poetry Review – "Friday Nights, 1968"
Cahoodaloodaling – "Politics, 1960"
Car Poems: A Collective Vehicle – "Unlicensed Driver"
Cincinnati Writers' Project – "The Lonely Game"
Company of Women: Chatter House Press – "In My First 50 Years," "Our Night Out," and "What She Taught Me"
First Jobs Series: Silver Birch Press – "Takin' Orders"
Flying Island – "Sunday Drive"
Hashtag Queer: LGBTQ+ Creative Anthology – "Her Name was Nancy," "Straight A's," and "I Wanted to be a Beatle"
Huron River Review – "Blank Sheet"
Ichabod's Sketchbook – "Unforgiven"
Pank – "The Day Truman Capote Died"
Poetry Breakfast – "Stuck in 'The Office'"
Rat's Ass Review – "Paying the Price"
Something's Brewing: Kind of a Hurricane Press – "Grounded in Coffee"
Tipton Poetry Journal – "In My New Apartment"
The Prose Poem Project – "Smothering Mother"
The Ramingo's Porch – "Love, Love, Love," and "Rewriting Romance"
Vacations: the Good, the Bad, & the Ugly: Outrider Press – "Witnesses in Wisconsin"
Weathering Under the Cat: Finishing Line Press – "For the Love of Cats"
Wilderness House Review – "Cruising, 1975," and "Some Memories Are Better Than Others"
Writer's Digest 75th Competition – HM – "Oh, Frank O'Hara!"

I would also like to thank my daughters, Keli and Alison, all my grandchildren, Codey, Carissa, Kyli, Alex, Scotty, Damon, Kolby, Colton, and my cats, Fiyero, Tink, and Styx for being the constant love in my life.

Contents

Influential Relationships (Family)

- My Loyal Friends 3
- For the Love of Cats 4
- At Grandma's House 5
- Friday Nights, 1968 6
- Smothering Mother, ... 7
- The Lonely Game 8
- Picture Perfect on my 4th Birthday 9
- Tomboy Pantoum 10
- Politics, 1960 11
- Weekends, 1967, At My Uncle's Pizza King, ... 12
- My Last Bottle 13
- Giving Up a Chick 14
- Stranger in My House 15
- Sunday Afternoons 16
- Grounded in Coffee 17
- On Thanksgiving 18
- Backyard Incident, 1961 19
- No Swimming 20
- The Stubborn Perfectionist 21
- Sunday Drive 22
- Shadow Warrior 23
- Puzzle 24
- Heart Trouble 25
- Lyle Rubush…Killed by a Train 26
- Invisible Child 27
- Stuck in "The Office" 29
- What You Wanted 30

Consequential Relationships
(Friends, Lovers, Teachers, Others)

Unforgiven 33
I Wanted to Be a Beatle 34
Straight A's 35
Her Name was Nancy 36
Lunchtime Bully 37
7th Grade Party, 1969 38
Music Quitter 39
Unlicensed Driver 40
Takin' Orders 41
Driven 43
At Eighteen 44
Cruising, 1975 45
Some Memories Are Better Than Others 46
Kurt Vonnegut Summer (or How I Spent My Summer Vacation) 47
Oh, Frank O'Hara! 49
After Our Candlelit Dinner 50
Witnesses in Wisconsin 51
In the Heart of Insomnia 52
Virgos 53
Our Night Out 54
Love, Love, Love 55
Living Single in Toledo 56
A Couple of Reborn Cynics 57
What She Taught Me 58
Here's the Church 60
Blank Sheet 61

Red Flag Relationships
(Warnings Everywhere)

- Lasting Impressions 65
- Unsettling Laughter 66
- Holding on to Me 67
- Dangerous Curves 68
- The Day Truman Capote Died 70
- The Last Time I Was Here 71
- Her Perceptions 72
- Alone in a Crowd 73
- Weddings 74
- Relationships and Red Flags 75

Hopeful Relationships
(Love Still Tries to Crack My Lock)

- In My New Apartment 79
- Surprise! 80
- Rewriting Romance 81
- My Heart Re-learns How to Ride 82
- Paying the Price 83
- Unrequited Crush 84
- Fragments 85

Influential Relationships
(Family)

2

My Loyal Friends

On the brown davenport,
lined up in my Virgo-ized order,

they looked at me in stuffed anticipation.
What would I tell them today?

What words could I cast them
to say to one another? What scenarios

could they play out
in the imagination of this only child?

An eight-year-old whom no one encouraged
to pursue her dreams of being

an art teacher or a guitar player
like John, Paul, or George.

No one to play games with except raggedy,
worn-out "Bobo" bear, or my favorite black cat –

"Inky" sported an ugly button sewn on
for his missing eye, and a well-worn

dolly shirt intended for blue Chatty Cathy,
because I preferred these animals, not dolls.

We were misfits in a white ranch
house in a small, Indiana, bland town –

where I lived "to be seen and not heard"
inside that quiet home with my fabricated friends:
 Yogi Bear, Huckleberry Hound, Quick Draw McGraw,
Baba Louie, and Cecil the Sea serpent

that really said, "Please give me a hug!" and
"I'll save you" when I pulled his string,

but no one knows what we witnessed inside
those lonely walls and the secrets we told each other.

For the Love of Cats

As a child I begged my dad, "let me have a cat"
and for years he never answered.
In the meantime, for my kitty fix, I visited cats
from my neighborhood, and checked out cat library books.

As an adult I faced lovers who hated cats –
an ex-husband who hated cats so much that whenever he saw one
near the road he gunned the car to hear me scream. After the divorce
I let my young daughters choose their first cat, Scribbles, and
we collected cats until we had Bo, Jonathon, Katie, Vic, and Ms. P.

My girls grew up and moved, and our cats lived out their lives
with me. But still, with cats in tow, I moved in with one lover
who threw Bo up against the wall for keeping her awake.
Another could not accept my cats sleeping in our bed,
she believed purring was growling, and hated cat fur.

Now, I live in a small house with my two black cats, siblings
Graham and Tink. We live in constant companionship – with no one
to threaten or shout when one of my cats lies on top of the refrigerator,
licks tuna salad from my plate, and drinks water in the kitchen sink.

At Grandma's House
For Gina

Over at grandma's house we played *Mystery Date*.
The dreamy guy or the cool dude waited for me,
but for you the bum lurked behind that door always.

Too young and freaked, you'd chew two Tums
to sooth your worried stomach
before we could play twice.

You wanted to be princess forever or prom queen.
We both liked the Beatles. I loved George,
you preferred John. We played air guitars and sang

"She loves you, yeah, yeah, yeah," over and over
and over again. Only we found giggles in repeating
"Oranges, poranges, who says?"

in our wicked renditions of Witchypoo.
I remember you, me, and Little Ben playing *Mod Squad*.
We called him "Chiefy" making him cry,

like he did when we'd play with Barbie dolls,
and run down his Skipper doll with Tonka trucks.
We'd get so loud grandma would clutch her chest,

go lay in her bed; her eyes closed, and shoes still on.
We took turns tip-toeing to her bedroom door –
breathless – to see if her chest moved.

We always thought we'd killed her.

Friday Nights, 1968

After barbeque
sausage pizza
with Barq's
Cream Soda,
grandpa stretched
in his green recliner
while grandma sat
in her red rocker,
both turned
towards the TV
and not each other.

Grandpa's long fingers
curled around his
cherry pipe bowl, filled
with Half & Half tobacco,
grandma's small hand
around her crystal barrel
glass filled with Coca-Cola.

On the small screen –
High Chaparral captured
their attention
as the cowpokes drove cattle
across Arizona Territory –
every Friday night episode,
held their small-town lives together,
Indiana lassoed and branded.

Smothering Mother,

remember when you forced me to sit on that red stool for hours. You pushed and pulled my hair into ringlets. I squirmed in your firm "hold still!" You made me wear dresses and patent leather shoes, and never let me swing upside down on monkey bars. I stayed in my room, listened to stacks of 45s, read Nancy Drew, and confided in stuffed Huckleberry Hound and Bugs Bunny. My school friends were not allowed in our house: Jackie too plump and Janet too wild for Church Street where Shirley Temple ruled. But that day when Mrs. Gannon, fat with religion, came to our door, I listened to her scold you for not allowing me to jump rope in her yard you thought was filled with mangy cats and dead grass. At home you called her mussed-up daughters "Edie, Audey, and Ugly." I hated when they called me "Curly" in public. Outside, her children played filthy with laughter, while I sat "ladylike" somber, inside.

The Lonely Game

As an only child I was thrilled
when Susie came over
to play. She never stayed
as long as I wanted. Doctor,
cops and robbers, hide and
seek could never keep her
from saying "I have to go
home." She promised always
to "be right back," and
every time I believed her.

On the front porch I sat,
on that small, silver milk box,
waiting for the sight of her
blond hair bouncing, plaid
pedal pushers, and a smile
running towards me and
I would watch for hours until
the porch lights came on and
mom called: "Come inside,
we'll play 'Old Maid.'"
I sat still watching fireflies
pretend hide and seek.

Picture Perfect on my 4th Birthday

I've always been uncomfortable getting my picture taken,
and it all started when I was really young –
but I had to get used to it as an only child,
my photo snapped constantly, even on the potty chair.

It all started when I was really young,
"look into the camera and 'say cheese!'"
My picture snapped constantly even on the potty chair,
my face grimaced and my small finger pointing, "stop!"

"Look into the camera and 'say cheese!'"
I didn't feel like smiling pretty every time –
my face grimaced and my small finger pointing, "stop!"
All I cared about was my birthday cake and presents.

I didn't feel like smiling pretty every time.
I felt silly in those dreadful Shirley Temple curls.
All I cared about was my birthday cake and presents,
not being the center of everyone's attention.

I felt so silly in those dreadful Shirley Temple curls,
but I had to get used to as an only child –
being the center of everyone's attention,
uncomfortable even when getting my picture taken.

Tomboy Pantoum

I was an always tomboy - a trait that troubled frilly mom:
I fought having to wear dresses every day to school –
back in those days it was the rule for all little girls,
all sugar and spice and everything nice I didn't find cool.

I fought wearing dresses every day to school –
I was stubbornly late to elementary classes quite often,
all sugar and spice and everything nice I didn't find cool,
I loved corduroy slacks and my favorite blue plaid shirt.

I was stubbornly late to elementary classes quite often,
so, the principal gave in and let me wear slacks under my dress.
I loved corduroy slacks and my favorite blue plaid shirt,
easier to run fast, play kickball, shoot hoops or marbles in.

The principal gave in and let me wear slacks under my dress.
Still, mom forced me into sewing instead of photography in 4H.
But I wanted to run fast, play kickball, shoot hoops or marbles –
no prissy girl bobbin threading or cutting silly fabric patterns for me!

Still, mom forced me into sewing instead of photography in 4H.
She didn't care that I won at steelies, beating the boys at their games,
no prissy girl bobbin threading or cutting silly fabric patterns for me,
collecting dolls, ribbons and barrettes, or wearing patent leather shoes.

She didn't care that I won at steelies, beating the boys at their games.
Back in those days it was the rule for all little girls:
collecting dolls, ribbons and barrettes, wearing those patent leather shoes.
I was an always tomboy - a trait that troubled frilly mom.

Politics, 1960

My earliest memory of politics
is of my vocal mom rooting for Nixon
over Kennedy. At four years old,
I wasn't interested in black and white
debates or adult talk about Catholics
or The Cold War.

Instead I sat in
the kitchen, on the floor,
beside Petey's birdcage, listening
to his cheerful chirps and
admiring many shades of blue color.

After the election,
I cringed hearing mom
tell everyone, over and over:
*The day Kennedy won, our TV
went kaput, and the parakeet died.*

Weekends, 1967, At My Uncle's Pizza King,

Gina and I, pressed plastic cups against the wall as if we were secret agents like Number Six in *The Prisoner,* or Maxwell Smart and Agent 99 in *Get Smart,* and listened to Taylor University students. Stationed inside her dad's office, we spied on the unsuspecting targets on the other side of the brown paneled wall in the dining room, packed, after a big game. They talked football, classes, who was dating who, and laughed loud often. We desperately wanted to be them, all grown up, independent. Practically living at the restaurant, we knew most of these guys. Tom, Dave, and Bob, were three of our favorites. Gina thought they were dreamy and hoped one would wait for her until she was old enough to date. I thought they were handsome and wanted to be athletic and popular like they were. Our cover was never blown, our silly giggles drowned out by songs on the juke box: "Kind of a Drag," "Dedicated to the One I Love," and "Light My Fire," fueling our youthful change.

My Last Bottle

I learned early and swiftly:
my inherent stubbornness
has consequences.

In bed for an afternoon nap,
mom had given me my bottle.
I'd grown attached to it, forming

a bad habit while enjoying my formula.
Old enough to know right
from wrong, I had been warned.

Yet, there was nothing like taking
a strand of my curly hair, wrapping
it around the nipple, and sucking.

It didn't bother me that my hair
was sticky, that ritual made me
happy and content. That day,

mom said if she *caught me doing it again,
that was it.* I must not have believed her.
Out of sight, I proceeded as usual –

and she re-appeared at the door.
I warned you! She yelled, coming at me
with purpose, yanking the bottle out of my hands,

and my sticky strands of hair. I lay crying
as she stomped off; helpless, I heard
my bottle crash into the garbage can.

Giving Up a Chick

When I was born, Uncle Ben was 15 years old
for four more days, making me a Virgo,
instead of his Libra. But I was his little companion
when I became a toddler and he could drive –
it's said that he never left the house without me
in the car. He drew pictures of bears in blue

ink that left an impression on me. He bought me
BB Bats, Kits, and Dum-Dums at the corner
drugstore. Once he drove me to Murphy's
Five and Dime in Hartford City close to Easter,
there were baby chicks for sale inside
a large, wired coop on the hardwood floor.

I wanted one so bad. Laughing, he let me
pick one for my own to take home. Happy and
holding my fuzzy yellow baby, I couldn't wait
for the chick to share my room. Not knowing

Uncle Ben knew his older sister, my mom,
would throw a clucking fit. She forced me
to give my new baby up to the neighbor
boy across the street – without visitation.

Stranger in My House

When I heard my mom say, "Go ask your dad,"
my stomach fluttered like dry leaves in a whirlwind.
"I can't," I replied.
"Oh, you can too, he's your father!" she said.

I looked for a way to extricate myself, but I'm trapped
in a Formica filled and mahogany house, with no white picket fence.

My legs quake as I stand in front of him,
dread pumps through my veins and exits my eyes,
sandpaper replaces my tongue as cracked words tumble from my lips.

"Can I have…a kitten…daddy?"
"Dad…can you put…a basketball goal up…for me?"
"Can I …borrow the…car keys?"

He sits still, and looks past me
out into the distant space,
my words fall silent,
a child not seen or heard.

I turn away, my heart pounding in hand,
serenading my insecure soul
as my sorry child chants
Never, never, never again…

Now, when I hear my mom's "I don't think you spoke to your father,"
I permit my eyes to look past him into my distant place.

Sunday Afternoons

Sometimes the loneliness inside my childhood home lingers –
those feelings of dread, screaming silence, nothing to do but
entertain make believe conversations with my stuffed animals,
listening to the same stack of 45s, reading many books I already read,
read more over and over. Sunday afternoons were the worst – that
eerie way the muted light reflected inside our house, no Captain
Kangaroo or cartoons on TV, nobody talking to each other, no pets
to play with, our house a place where all dreams went to die.

Grounded in Coffee

Its sweet aroma
brings back the grinding aisles
of a small Indiana A & P,
where I shopped with mom and grandma –
JFK was president, I was into Captain Kangaroo,
hula hoops, and Quick Draw McGraw.
When we visited Aunt Dot's, in Russiaville,
the always coffee pot was on. She and my dad,
and any number of their ten siblings,
would sit around the kitchen table and adult talk
while I played Life, or Yahtzee, with many cousins.
After the 3rd pot of coffee was gone it was time to go home.
In those days, back home mom made me drink dreaded milk.
With supper over, dad went to his easy chair, mom to her dishes,
and I sat at the deserted kitchen table –
that glass of milk turning my stomach
as it grew warmer by the hour, I imagined curly hairs or
tiny ants or worms in the bottom of the glass.
Stubborn, I refused even a sip.
My reluctant mom opened up
the Folger's jar, and after a spoonful
of instant coffee stirred into my lukewarm milk,
finally,
I tasted freedom.

On Thanksgiving

There would be grandma,
telling grandpa to wipe his chin;
mom and Uncle Ben arguing over
her green bean casserole –
he always called "scabs."
Grandma telling them to be nice
as if they were in their teens,
instead of their forties.

The windows steamed
as dead leaves whirred outside,
but the Midwest chill couldn't touch
the banter inside that kitchen.
After grandpa died in 1987,
grandma held on to her recipe
for food and family disharmony.
When she died in 1998, my mom
and uncle's playful arguing turned mean,
burying years of Thanksgiving memories
beneath piles of picked clean
and broken wish-bones.

Backyard Incident, 1961

I was playing in grandma's backyard
with Aunt Carolyn while she hung
wash on the clothesline

on a beautiful, sun-filled day,
its warmth and smell of clean
clothes a comfort –

until the neighbor's spider monkey
jumped the fence, ran towards us,
climbed on the clothesline and

pulled the pins off – like bombs,
shirts and towels dropped to the ground.
Aunt Carolyn screamed for him to scat.

Not surrendering his antics, and sporting
a face that looked like a tiny old man –
he laughed at our reactions.

An only child, at five years old,
I yearned for a playmate, but that tiny monkey
petrified me. For years afterwards

he hustled to grandma's backdoor and waited
patiently on the stoop for me to grow affection for him.
At times, Uncle Ben held me so I could see:

the monkey on the other side of the window
wouldn't hurt me. Instead I saw a menacing bully,
that a well-meaning uncle, or

years of sun-filled summers,
could never chase away.

No Swimming

I wish I knew how to swim instead of walking
nowhere on treadmills or lifting dumbbells

inside a drab gym to tone my middle-
aged muscles and slim my widening hips.

Why did I listen to my overcautious mom
and grandma warn of drowning and

ingest their tales of never learning to let go,
never handing control over to water bodies?

I never took a chance on surrendering
to water even when it waved and enticed me

into the shallow end, afraid it would push me
over my head deep, alive and smothering –

afraid to experience the euphoria of buoyancy.

The Stubborn Perfectionist

A lazy left eye
that never wandered
kept me focused enough
that it went unrecognized
for five years until
kindergarten round-up.

I flunked the eye test
and was sent to a doctor
who in those days remedied
with glasses and a patch
over my good eye –

Mom picked out girly pink cameo
frames, calling them cat eye
glasses didn't perk me up.
Playing pirate got old and
she even made me color
with the eye patch on.

When my coloring went outside
the lines, I scribbled hard across
the page and pitched the coloring
book across the room.

Soon, when the patch went on,
I'd throw myself on the couch,
shut my eyes and wait
for thirty minutes
to blindly go by.

Sunday Drive

In the backseat of our '66 green Pontiac Bonneville, my view was of the back of my parent's heads: dad with dark wavy hair, hands on the steering wheel, his pipe smoke swirling upward and back into my space; mom with coiffed hair, in the passenger's seat chewing her Juicy Fruit gum. I was along for the ride each Sunday going to see my grandma who lived an hour away in Kokomo. I loaded up the backseat with my favorite stuffed animals and a few books in hopes of making time cruise a bit faster. I hated leaving other beloved belongings behind, feeling guilty for all that couldn't go. I loved listening to the radio, Fort Wayne's strong AM station, WOWO. The Beatles, Neil Diamond, The Supremes, Tammy Wynette and George Jones were played one after the other. I could've done without country, but dad preferred it to my favorites. I sang along with all songs that came on, even D-I-V-O-R-C-E. Mom marveled how I knew every word, saying she wished I memorized my homework like I did those songs. I worried all new song lyrics would be used up by the time I became a mom, driving with my own kids riding in the backseat.

Shadow Warrior
to Kagemusha

I've never been to the Land of the Rising Sun,
where, long ago, a dishonored Samurai warrior
was duty bound to commit seppuku –

but I heard the stories about grandpa, drafted
flat footed into World War II, in his early thirties
and a family at home – he rode brave in Japan

in the back of Army trucks – a grub cook to American soldiers.
At night he listened to Tokyo Rose. After the war,
family members often teased him for having listened to her,

and for his getting love letters, while "over there,"
from a woman, not his wife, who wrote "sending you
oceans and oceans of love with a kiss on each wave."

Red faced, he'd force a smile, but he never joined in
his family's laughter. That's how he survived that war – far from home
to return a warrior, ripped to threads by his own flesh and blood.

How much of grandpa was stripped away
before he finally faded
into silhouette?

If he hadn't died at age seventy-six,
grandpa would be 100 years old next year.
How I wish he shared with me

the stories he carried back,
along with a Samurai sword –
buried deep within.

Puzzle

In those days my father sat at my little table
with me and my stuffed animals, his knees up to his chin,
sipping pretend tea, and putting puzzle pieces together.
I never thought those days would end.

Now retired, with two grandchildren and five great grandchildren,
he never sips pretend tea. Although he sits
for their soccer games and birthday wishes,
they puzzle his quiet ways and I pick up the pieces.

I would like to say to him, Why don't you open up?
Tell me what it was like when your father was found
run over by a train, on his way home to a pregnant wife,
twelve kids, and you just thirteen.

What was it like to quit school at sixteen
to support your mom and nine younger siblings?
What was it like in Korea – a war
that left you rice intolerant, purple heart scarred,
and too foreign for words?

Heart Trouble

I.
Before I was ever thought of
my two grandmas lost their true loves
in violent ways. My paternal grandpa,
Lyle, run over by a freight train –

rumor was: someone robbed him
and laid him unconscious on the tracks.
My patient grandma waited
supper at home, with their twelve
hungry kids, the thirteenth due any day.

What are the odds of a woman
in 1940s America finding another man –
another chance at love with all that baggage?
Cecil never married again, and
raised a restless thirteen on her own.

When I was twelve, my paternal grandma died
after surviving years and years of heart trouble,
her seventh heart attack the final blow.

II.
On their way to a church basketball game,
my maternal grandma and her fiancé,
Harold, were tossed out of a car
they were riding in. Her head split open,
he didn't get needed attention at the scene
for keeping his injuries internal.

Marjorie Dean married Clayton,
my grandpa, after meeting on a blind date
years after she survived the accident –
Harold still in her heart, after fifty still years
of marriage, and two children.

Grandma outlived grandpa by eleven years –
never wanting another man in her life, weary
as grandpa's caregiver for many years after
a major stroke, tolerating his childlike tantrums,
dodging his cane from the next poke or blow.

Lyle Rubush...Killed by a Train

Grandpa was run over by a train
It was something dad never talked about, and
I knew not to question. What little I knew
of the train tragedy, I overheard
from uncles, aunts or young cousins.
Two versions followed me through my youth:
He was on his way home from work,
walking on train tracks and didn't hear
the train. This story stuck: he was robbed,
hit over the head, laid on the tracks, and
when found his watch and rings were gone.
No matter, the one constant was my grandma
pregnant with Aunt Audra, their thirteenth child.
His death derailed the family of an easy destination.

The truth arrived unexpectedly, January 2017.
My dad, 86, ill and in the hospital. Cousins in
constant contact, I was given the newspaper link
to the information when grandpa was killed
June 6th, 1943, dad just 13 years old.
Through my tears, I read:

> *Sharpsville Man Struck by Nickel Plate Early Sunday.*
> *Body Badly Mangled. 42-year-old father of twelve*
> *was killed instantly at 3:40 o'clock Sunday morning...*
> *Rubush was sitting on the rail at the time of the fatal accident.*
> *[the] conductor of the train, saw Rubush on the track*
> *but too late to stop the train. The train was moving*
> *approximately 45 miles an hour. It was raining...*
> *...no immediate explanation as to why the man was sitting*
> *on the track at the time of the accident or how he got there.*

Now, when train whistles whine and I hear the rumbling
force of those steel wheels rolling along the tracks
they signal an even sadder, distant familial connection.

Invisible Child

Growing up I was told:
"Children should be seen, not heard" –
I knew to be quiet, no rowdy outbursts,
no arguing with mom –
 dad didn't like "loud." The reason
always given: I'm the only child.

Most think "only" means spoiled,
getting everything wanted,
being doted on and loved.
My parents went out of their way
making sure I didn't fit that mold.

Begging for attention, always trying
to be the best, never validated
at home for my solo poem recital
at kindergarten graduation, first place
art award in 3rd grade, high school
art scholarships. Instead, mom said,
"You're too creative for your own good."

I became important when boys
came calling. Excited Mom asked,
"Where did you go…and how far?"
I never married the right man –
at eighteen it was to get out of the house;
at thirty because I was still nothing without a man,
at thirty-two another poor choice
giving in to aging doubts.

When I came out at thirty-eight,
mom called it a phase, then blamed herself.
She hated my first girlfriend, who freaked
mom's mind with combat boots, a Mohawk, and chains.
Degree by degree, I came into my own, gaining
respect and writing my way into belonging.

At fifty-five a published poet,
an educator, respected by peers, colleagues, friends.
Mom calls and asks, "What's new?"
Never waits for an answer, instead she talks
about this man or that, who's lost weight, her cats, and
I disappear.

Stuck in "The Office"

The office is where
my young cousins and I
were shooed off to
whenever the restaurant
got too busy on a weekend
night after a ball game
that brought in hoards
of youth…not much older
than we were…for pizza
and pop, sometimes
the works of everything
out of the fountain, called
a "suicide."

If we were not sent to
that office, we could get
run down by the teens
pouring into the hottest
restaurant in town, or
burnt by the busy pizza
paddles lifting those pies
in and out of the huge Bunn
ovens, or we could accidentally
trip a waitress carrying
trays full of drinks to
thirsty athletes or cheerleaders.

We always wanted
to be part of the action,
inside that office we could
hear the roar of voices,
the laughter, the excitement
of a world going on without
us…and I wonder if that's why
the appeal of being holed up
in an office as an adult seems
more like a prison than a
place that I really want to be.

What You Wanted

Mother, remember my Kindergarten teacher, Mrs. Johnson,
so impressed with my drawing skills she called you in to see?
I loved the attention, the excitement of someone noticing me.
My talent or recognition didn't matter – that's not what you wanted
for me. Was I staying in line, behaving like a good girl?

Mrs. Johnson asked me to memorize a poem
for kindergarten graduation, you argued I couldn't.
There are pictures of me reciting that poem, front and center
stage in my small cap and gown. How I wish I remembered
more about that poem, it was about the seasons. You never
bothered to write the title down or say I made you proud.

In third grade, I won first place in the class art contest.
You weren't thrilled. I should be trying harder in math,
a subject I struggled with. In junior high, it was boys.
In high school I caught the eye of the art teacher, another
Mrs. Johnson, who marveled at my drawing skills - you doubted it.

I won first place in pottery, she kept my polka horse print and my heart,
sculpted in clay, with my permission. I earned the right to attend
John Herron Art School Saturday classes in Indianapolis. You were
more interested in what boys were there. You schooled me to "play the field,"

to date around. My goal should be to get married: marry a doctor, a rich man,
or maybe the local mechanic with those large biceps. You would love
to welcome him into the family. A man is what you ultimately wanted
for me – never impressed with the real me: your talented daughter.

Consequential Relationships
(Friends, Lovers, Teachers, Others)

Unforgiven

When I was in first grade I fell into my first-grade classroom unforgiven,
I tripped flat forward and my lunch tray flew across the floor,
my face turned red and I was called a klutz,
I never forgot the jeering laughter.

That same year I dropped and broke my Magic 8 Ball in the gym.
It never predicted its own black gooey death.
I had to sit with my head on my desk, face down, ink well collecting tears.
Will I ever forget my sins of first grade?

My teacher that year was Aunt Gertie who expected my perfection.
I got in trouble for dragging my feet in the merry-go-round mud,
she called my mom to bring in clean shoes and socks, to get rid of my filth.
I never forgot the shaming looks.

I made easy friends with a rural boy with a hair lip and his twin sister,
and learned that there are those you friend and those you don't –
my adults pointed out every friend's faults: too ugly, too dirty, too fat, too poor.
I never forget to second guess my choices.

I Wanted to Be a Beatle

It wasn't because
I was in love
with Paul or George,
Ringo or John like most girls,
or one of the screaming young
women who desperately
wanted to marry one of them.

At eight years old,
I would go to bed
at night, lie awake and
think what it would be like
for those girls to love me
so much they'd chase after me,
scream for me, feel the need
to touch my face, my hair,
my clothes.

Straight A's

The year The Beatles invaded America,
my second-grade teacher, Miss Emswiller,
shared my love of the Fab Four.
She brought Beatle card gum packets to school
and gave them to my friend, Kim, and me.
She let us stay inside during recess,
listening to us gush and sing their songs,
she laughing with us. I knew I was a favorite –
she never gave me a bad grade in math,
I passed her class with flying colors.

My wrong math got red marked in third grade,
cutting into my straight A's. Upset, my mom searched
my second-grade math workbooks for clues. She found
I had not been corrected when I put 2+2=5 or 2+2=8.
For years I struggled with numbers –
equations that didn't add up.
As I grew older, I'd see Miss Emswiller and her always sister
together – biking, walking, shopping, never a man in sight.
I never held it against my second-grade teacher,
though mom accused her of ruining my relationship with math.
She wasn't pleased when I did learn to put 2+2 together,
and finally came out.

Her Name was Nancy

My first crush when I was 10 –
she worked at my uncle's restaurant.
She was beautiful, with the prettiest
brown eyes. Every time "Brown-eyed
Girl" came on the radio, I felt warm
all over. I didn't wonder why or
worry these feelings were wrong.

With my own Brownie camera,
I wanted a picture of her – too shy to ask,
I acted like I wanted pictures of my
two little cousins, and called Nancy over,
"Get in the picture!" Then, innocently,
"Just one of you?"

I loved that black and white photograph,
her in that waitress mini-skirt, and
tight white top, standing outside
of the restaurant, in front of my uncle's
'66 silver Corvette Stingray
convertible. How she shined.

Lunchtime Bully

In fourth grade I encountered
an unlikely bully. I remember
her name to this day, but out of fear
I'll refrain from using it. She was
a quiet girl, much bigger than me, and
super religious – her slick dark hair
pulled into a ponytail and always
those long dresses.

She cornered me in the classroom,
after others had filed out to the cafeteria,
and forced me to hand over my sack lunch –
my peanut butter and jelly sandwich,
Ruffles potato chips and
milk money.

Always hungry at lunch, but knowing
I should share, I'd offer her half of what I had.
Bully she was, she wanted it all, plus any loose change
I might have in my pockets for my afternoon
chocolate milk.

She would punch me in the stomach or twist my arms
until I felt they would break like twigs, or worse
she'd threaten to tell the teacher that I'd done
something I hadn't.

I never wanted to get into trouble –
Mrs. Myers wielding that wicked paddle,
the troublemaker touching toes, waiting for wood
decorated with holes to raise stinging welts.

So, stomach growling, I'd go through those days,
missing afternoon milk after recess,
while my bully sat smiling and
full of herself.

7th Grade Party, 1969

It was a Friday night
boy-girl party
at Sharon's house.
She was a preacher's daughter,
so mom allowed me to go.

Locked in
her dark bedroom,
Steve pushed me down
onto the bed, laid on top of me
and kissed me hard with tongue.

Although others were outside
the bedroom door laughing,
I fought him off, not thinking it funny,
I felt dirty and afraid. I felt sick.
I left the party, walked down the alley

to my grandparent's house.
My parents were working
at my uncle's restaurant.
I found my grandparents
in their normal routine.

Grandma washing dinner dishes,
drinking a Coke. Grandpa in his recliner,
watching TV, smoking his pipe.
I was not normal anymore.

With guilt I asked my beloved grandma.
Can girls get pregnant from kissing?

Her usual loving tone with me changed:
Why would you ask something like that?
I shrunk. I couldn't tell her a boy kissed me
so hard it hurt. I worried for weeks
in virgin territory....

Music Quitter

      I

In fourth grade, I learned song flute,
which made me want to learn a major
music instrument to play in school band.
Mom chose the flute for me – more ladylike,
and inexpensive. Blowing across its opening
made me dizzy. I hated the flute. I refused it

wanting to try something else. Mom decided
clarinet, my older cousin excelled with one.
She impressed mom since she won Delaware County
4H Fair Queen and was head high school cheerleader.

We traded the flute in for a clarinet. I learned
to change the reeds, but was frustrated when
I tended to always make the reeds squeak.
Practicing this wind instrument was boring,
so it stayed in its case day in and day out.

I quit band, but Mr. McKinley, the band teacher,
wanted me to succeed. I met with him afternoons
and he let me try out different instruments –
drums were off limits to me since I was a girl.
The instrument I took to was the trombone.

Even he said I had a knack for it, I could
make that horn honk and moan. When we
approached mom with my joyful news, she said, "No."
I'd had my chance with music. I wasn't going to go
through every instrument known.

      II

At the end of junior high I wasn't interested in school band –
I wanted to start a band of my own. I needed a guitar.
Again, mom said, "No," but at the factory dad made a deal
with a guy selling his electric guitar and amplifier. I began guitar
lessons right away, with ease I learned the chords and boasted
blistered fingers. I wanted to play pop songs like a pro, it wasn't
as easy as I hoped. When the guitar teacher's son asked me out,
at fourteen, the guitar and the amplifier took a back seat.

Unlicensed Driver

My first memory of driving
was around 15 –
I was waitressing
at my uncle's restaurant.

Mom, dad, my aunt and
uncle had gone home
early for an adult party
later that evening.

My two younger cousins
assigned to stay with me,
were to be brought
home by our designated driver –

Bill, a policeman
already drinking,
was ready
for that party in Eaton;

he continued to drink
but didn't want to drive,
so he told me I had to.
I was excited to drive

8 miles on real [rural] roads
but scared of him –
hovering [always] at 6'7" and
unusually gruff. This night

he resembled a jolly giant,
as he instructed me to "get
behind the wheel" of his [rusty]
red Jeep, laughing at how mad

my parents would be. Livid
they were; yet, we all made it
home safe; me yearning
to drive again and again.

Takin' Orders

When *Ms. Fish-on-a-Plate* came
in wielding her walker and wearing
those thick Coke bottle glasses
we knew her order
before she even sat down.
When she complained
about her coffee
being cold again, We'd grumble.
  if she'd drink it when
  we took it to her
  it'd still be hot.
The *Ironing Board Lady*
was also a regular who *we said* looked
freshly pressed from *her man of the week,*
  her make-up so gaudy,
  her bright red lips
  left kisses on the coffee cups.
Frank, *The Juke Box Man* changed out 45s
  for more popular ones
  that'd get more spins,
Ms. Sarge O'Pork
danced under the air vent
singing, *All I need is The Air that I Breathe…*
as she cooled off
from working the hot pizza ovens.
Funny guy, John, called out my orders for *Lula Belle,*
LaLa, Molasses, or *Lyle…* to pick up and take
to hungry customers. After the ball games
the roar of voices over the jukebox blaring:
  Old black water…keep on rolling… Or,
  Saturday night's alright, alright, alright…
  well they're packed pretty tight
  here tonight…,

while we juggled peperoni pizzas, trays of Pepsi,
Mountain Dew, and "Suicides," whipping through crowds
of other untamed youth. Happy at 2 a.m. to hang
that closed sign, and laugh our way through clean-up
on those busy weekends:

>teenagers working for food,
>small tips, and time spent with each other
>at my uncle's restaurant,
>when coffee was a dime, and
>cops got served for free.

Driven

At 16, I test drove a '57 Chevy, the car
that flares in the back – like wings.
It was turquoise and white and didn't
have power steering. It was hard
for my young arms to turn.

So, my first car was a 1964 Buick
Skylark Convertible, white exterior and
red vinyl seats and dashboard.
My parents bought the car
from twenty-three-year-old Terry –
a licentious grease monkey
who took me for a test drive
in the country and a spin
I wouldn't forget.

That car and Terry
shifted my life –
one would leave me
stranded on train tracks or in the middle
of busy intersections, one would leave me
directionless on a well-traveled road,
empty, fueled with doubts.

At Eighteen
After Edward Hirsch's "At Sixteen"

I walked out of the white Formica house and into fire,
past myself down the dim, long aisle
where scores of women had gone before.
I quit my waitress job at uncle's restaurant.

I walked past myself down the dim, long aisle.
My mother nudged me along the way.
I missed waitressing at uncle's restaurant,
where I ate the attention of other waitresses.

My mother nudged me along the way.
My husband didn't like the way I held my fork.
I ate the attention of other waitresses.
Everyone laughed at my expense.

My husband didn't like the way I held my fork.
He wanted to own me like his custom '69 Corvette.
Everyone laughed at my expense.
I wanted him gone so I chewed up my tongue.

He wanted to own me like his custom '69 Corvette.
I painted a picture of a woman turning worry into wine.
I wanted him gone so I chewed up my tongue
and got a job loading ovens at a glass factory.

I painted a picture of a woman turning worry into wine.
I walked out of the white Formica house and into fire,
stuck loading ovens at a glass factory,
where scores of women had gone before.

Cruising, 1975

We drove the small-town strip in Bill's Corvette,
from the carwash on the north side and around

the A & W Root Beer stand, next to the cornfield,
back and forth on State Road 3, going nowhere.

I sang "Love Will Keep Us Together," out loud,
even though I knew it wasn't love. I felt safe

with Bill who wasn't like the small-town policeman
who violated my virginity when I was fifteen.

In the rearview mirror – reflections of a female friend,
in her small Vega with a bronze body, made my heart skip.

Oblivious of the implications, Bill and I revved our drive-by
love – eight years and two daughters away from a divorce,

racing towards a lifetime linked by grandchildren and silent
stares, two strangers who tried to drive their dreams home.

Some Memories Are Better Than Others

A midnight Kenny Rogers cuts in
Lady, I'm your knight in shining armor…
2009 fades into 1980 and I'm married
to still Bill who says I don't stir
spaghetti sauce right. He hurls
pottery I made to the floor, and accuses
me of holding our baby daughter too much:
"She'll grow up to be lesbian." He swears
I won't leave him, no one else will love me.
He killed my plans with women, friends I loved
before him. My philandering fear
chewed and swallowed what he dished.
I sat at the table beside myself,
digesting raw conversation,
when aversion finally belched.
Bill bellowed, "You're as spineless as boiled shrimp!"
In a saucy moment I shot his malicious words down
faster than Dick Cheney on a quail hunt,
and served him
marriage leftover stew. A delicious recipe
that slowly simmers and spurns.

Kurt Vonnegut Summer
(or How I Spent My Summer Vacation)

Spring swallows sunset
summer dawns
alarm blares   6 a.m.
another draining day
toiling for   dollars
already spent,
so it goes.
Stealing Vonnegut
moments   sating
my appetite with
Breakfast of Champions,
watching ducks waddle
towards pond
before punching
time clock –
Welcome to the Monkey House,
windowless,
tongues wagging
keeping time
cats climbing
escaping deckled edges…
Where's Billy Pilgrim now?
Independence day
rolls around
blow out I-69
southbound Indianapolis
"Six dykes in this van
and only one knows
how to change a tire?"
Chris saves the day,
fireworks, cake, and
she moves away.
Jen sits
her parasol down.
I check out
Cat's Cradle.
Shan and Pete
prefer Ann Rice,
although Chi town
is really nice…

Is Kilgore Trout here?
We must have
missed him
when we turned
on Halsted.
At work, more tails
wagging on the wall,
how I don't want
to be here at all.
Pendulum moments
Hocus Pocus
vacation time
campfire spits
embers   Smoky
Mountain embrace
Jess smiles,
Cheryl sends
her love.
God Bless You, Mr. Rosewater.
Concerts resonate
Reba's sexy drawl
grows my heart
and various womyn
harmonize my soul
at Lilith Fair.
Handmade paper
wraps around
my fingers
creative craft
makes money,
not enough...
Alarm blares   6 a.m.
summer spews
kaleidoscope colors
autumn swallows summer.
Another draining day
toiling for dollars
already spent,
so it goes.

Oh, Frank O'Hara!

July 1996, two months shy of my 40th year,
I sit at MT Cup Café, reading City Poet
as society walks by, oblivious to me
realizing Frank was tossed fast
as if he were a crumpled revision
on Fire Island,
just two months shy of my 10th year, July 1966,
leaving pages staring blank, waiting
to be filled with his lunch poems, biting humor
and city sass in his 40th year.

Years, I sated my hunger
by swallowing Frank's lunch poems
whole, digesting "Cornkind" to nourish
my "Steps," feasting on"St. Paul and All That," picking bones
and trimming fat, inspiring "I do this, I do that," life lines
as tight as "Mary Desti's Ass,"
and dream July 2006, two months shy of my 50th year,

where I sit at Carpo's café, formerly the San Remo,
drinking in city sass, 1950s reflections
of neon and exhaust etching my plate
full, juicy jazz spreading into spicy lines and enjambing
my thoughts over my blank pages, like gravy
soaking up dry stanzas, coating my libido
wet with words! oh, god it's wonderful
the metaphors mixed and syntax sangria!

After Our Candlelit Dinner

We cruise down
the road,
Annie Lenox
Diva on deck   stars
glide in and out
of my eyes as you
drive, we smile
we talk, we laugh
you slip your hand
into mine, fingers
interlock like genius
puzzle pieces.
My heart quickens,
body muscles thrust
like when ascending
roller coaster reaches
peak   anticipating
your kiss.

Caught up in moment
you find a dark
intimate country lane
we pull in   lights out
our clothes melt
into floorboards
as our kisses steam
glass   isolates
us into our burning world
as my feelings
for you gush
onto your fingers,
I feel your warmth
so soft   so moist
I lick your lips
and know
this is where
I will dwell forever.

Witnesses in Wisconsin

We witnessed the sun's last gasp in Wisconsin,
smothered by scruffy clouds headed south
in a hurry, as we traveled north
bound to friends in Fort Atkinson.

Sirens warned us, surrounded
by Mother Nature's twisted escapees,
armed and dangerous – who tip cows,
ransack houses and toss cars for thrills.

We were hostage, blinded by rain
and cursed with hail, easy targets
for apple shrapnel and fallen tree bazookas.

Too late to change our course. No turn –
ing back. We had to reach Sandy and Brian's,
safe on Rock River's bank,
where laughter rolls,
good food flows as cats grow to our laps,
and on clear nights we watch
fireflies burn the moon,
flickering glitter upon the water.

In the Heart of Insomnia

In the Heart of the Heart of the Country
                -- William H. Gass

It's the heart of winter, two a.m.
in the heart of Indiana,

in the heart of the bed,
Maggie snuggles next to me

deeply breathing her dreams,
and I'm on the edge

listening to freezing rain chatter
February on our window pane,

low flying jets,
gliding west at three-thirty a.m.,

trains whistle me awake.
weary words crisscross my mind,

form erratic lines in search of a poem,
I weave in and out of insomnia,

weathering under the cat
purring sleep across my belly.

Virgos
For Glenn

Imagine it! A couple of Virgos,
not prone to spontaneity,
deciding on a whim, to meet in Fort Wayne,
a midway rendezvous for two
friends leaving our partners
alone at home, and leaving others

to wonder about our 'affair.' A fair
curiosity since most associate one man and
one woman and one night in a motel with sex –
a gay man and a lesbian don't play hetero-sex-
ual, so get your minds out of the gutter!

Believe it! It's rare to find a friend
who shares an affinity for scheduling fun
months in advance, spending hours critically
analyzing why cats or politicians do
this or that. Still it's not fair to swear we Virgos
are too uptight to let loose for once –

critiquing each other's poems, laughingly
finding fault at how closely "wonton" and
"wanton" look, and where muscular ladies show up
by mistake in a line after too much wine. And, oh,
those two scheduled massages within the strip
mall on Lima Road with Chong Chong and Michelle –
sometimes it is better to "don't ask, don't tell!"

Our Night Out

In a dark bar on a Toledo Saturday,
too early for the happening crowd,
too late for two friends who decide to stay
in a place that pulls our memories
from "far-out" places – the music patronizes
our middle-age while still flirting with youth –
swigging liquid courage, musing over *Dancing
in the Dark,* and "Who's going to drive you home,
tonight?" Remembering loud nights
that didn't seem too long, way back when,
when we were not paying attention to time,
tick, tick, tocking forward. Our minds reflecting
refracting pieces of our disco selves unraveling
like an off track 8 track tape and when we twirl
around we see each other in the bar mirror –
cynical and dark.

Love, Love, Love

I laugh at the idea of love.
I hear Delilah on the radio schmoozing
with callers on her all night love fest
as I drive, from Indianapolis back home
to Toledo, passing the hours by listening to sappy
tales of romance – what a joke,
as I relive past loves with each love song
she spins into the air so sweetly.
I don't love the idea of love anymore –
this once hopeless romantic
truly has had enough of the "Silly Love Songs,"
like the ones that McCartney and Lennon sold
in catchy tunes for impressionable youths
to believe in the perfect love, the happy ever after,
the match made in heaven, the kind of romance that never ends,
"Love Me Do," "From Me to You," "Love, love, love…," and after all
the failed attempts at romance and wedded bliss,
I certainly don't "long for yesterday," or a late night
chat with the love seductress, Delilah.

Living Single in Toledo

Again, after months or more
of staying away, there's no convincing us
that the gay bar scene is going to be
bare and boring again. We always
share optimism in our cynicism:
surely there will be interesting, exciting
people to meet in worn-down
Toledo this time around. We can't be
the only living singles here. We are
smart, witty, and awesome,
looking for same –
Never mind that we're middle-aged and best friends.
One man and one woman –
in that way we are the epitome
of the conservative definition of marriage.
We are not interested in marriage ourselves.
All we want is a date, an enjoyable evening out
with someone of the same sex,
someone who is not so young they've never heard
of Tiddlywinks, or so old that they're only mobile in a Hoveround.
Tonight, with skeptical hope, we walk
into the gay bar that touts: "Dance Your Ass Off"
with their hip DJ at 10 PM - the dance floor dismal as our love lives.
After a few drinks, asses still on, we decide to try the lesbian bar
in hopes that it'd be hopping. We pull into the parking lot –
only two other cars. We don't bother to get out
of the third car. Instead we pull away,
and go to our homes before midnight strikes
us disenchanted, again.

A Couple of Reborn Cynics

Enough time has lapsed
and it's a Toledo gay bar
scene, Friday night.
"Rainy Days and Mondays"
Karen Carpenter's voice
booms – it's '70s on 7
Sirius XM, instead of live
music.

"It's just another day…"
McCartney sings,
Glenn cringes, turns
around, sees a table
full of hungry young men,
heads down, texting –
21st Century socializing.

The token lesbian couple
walk in – they come
to our table, say "hi,"
get drunk, get loud,
and fight. Again.

Tonight's special –
Grandma's Kool-aid,
we're sad we missed
karaoke night, as we sing
a bad rendition of "Total Eclipse
of the Heart." Glenn glares
at me, shakes his head –
says at least I'll have another
Toledo-sucks-poem.

We notice
the free buffet, and
no one is getting any –
unfortunate metaphor
of our lives.

What She Taught Me
For Ann Johnson

          I

If she hadn't been that teacher
who pushed me past my limits,
made me give a voice to purple,
in front of the class, who praised
my Polka Horse block print and
asked to keep it for her own,

who gave me unlimited hall passes
signed AJ, to ditch my dreaded Home Ec
at the end of the school day to come
to the art room, where no one cared
if I could sew a stitch, or sauté an onion.

If she hadn't been that teacher
who flunked me for not painting
by deadline, who teased me
out of my shell, who didn't turn me away
when I dropped by her house to say "hi,"
dressing so funky that
she didn't care who stared.

If she hadn't been that teacher
who was vibrant and different,
in school convocations, who dared
to show vulnerability, I would not have
kept going back to school,
each day a new reason to live.

She gave me opportunity to see some world
outside of rural Indiana, first Toronto,
then Niagara Falls, Buffalo, Chicago with art
club – a first airplane ride, a first
subway passage, a first time not feeling lost.

II
If she hadn't been that friend
saddened by my dropping out
of college to marry a man, then
a few years later helping me
get back into art by sharing shows to enter,
new techniques to try and didn't "I told you so"
when I told her I was filing for divorce.

If she hadn't been that friend
who gave me a job cutting and coating
handmade paper jewelry in her studio
so I could support myself and my
two young daughters,

who told me to drive during rush hour
in the heart of Chicago, who sent me to the MOMA alone,
while she manned the art booth in New York City,
who trusted me to drive her, after major surgery, to Twin Rocker
for handmade paper supplies, through blinding snow –
it wouldn't be our last trip through rough weather together
living through damning "Bible skies."

If she hadn't been that friend
who encouraged me to write poetry
when I doubted that I could, who spoke
of *Writing Down the Bones,* and suggested
over and over that I re-enroll in college
twenty years after I gave it up –

If she hadn't been the one –
strong, independent woman
who lead me by example:
accomplished artist, mother, teacher,
businesswoman, world traveler.
When I didn't believe
in me, she did.

Here's the Church

Here's the steeple...

I remember that handy game, glass
stained with sun, giving life to color
spectrums climbing the walls -
crossing over sepia portrait
of Jesus like the one that hung
in grandma's house on Church Street,
in great-grandpa's Methodist Church
where he ministered his flock
long before I was born.

Open the door

Two uncles became self-professed
ministers of their own brand of religion –
God-fearing, all fire and brimstone,
faith above all after years of abusing
alcohol, cussing long and loud, living
on the edge of hell. A cousin, who married
nine times, became ordained and performed
my final marriage to a man, eight years
before I finally came out.

Out run the people...

As a child, I loved Bible School.
I remember singing "Jesus Loves Me"
and believing. As a young adult
"O Little Town of Bethlehem,"
"Silent Night," and "Joy to the World,"
warmed me in the glow of candlelight
during Christmas Eve services.

Now, years since stepping foot inside
a church, I remember singing
hymns on Sunday and feeling
that I belonged.

Blank Sheet

As an artist
I can take
a blank sheet,
turn it into
anything –
larger-than-life faces,
some blue jay playing sax,
a crazy-looking cat –
my imagination
come to life.

As a poet
I can use
a blank sheet,
spin it with
words
that rhyme,
lines of love crimes
that commit phrases,
my words breathing
images on the page.

As a lover
I can't be
a blank sheet,
fresh as if I've
never been
hurt –
left behind love,
belittled, abused,
my worn heart
torn like discarded paper
full of filthy smudges.

Red Flag Relationships
(Warnings Everywhere)

Lasting Impressions

I was a senior at Delta
High School, a promising artist
whose sanctuary was room 14
where *Benny and the Jets, Rock On,*
and *The Loco-Motion* ruled
the air waves as I pulled colorful prints,
the relief I needed from
living life on the edge –

pressed into sexual encounters
with that small-town cop at fifteen.
The one who told me I was
no better than anyone else;
he swore *You're so Vain*
was about me. Who was I,
anyway, to think I was going
to breakout of this rural routine?

Killing me softly with his song...
He knocked me down a few notches
when he went to mom and told
her I was sleeping with a local
grease monkey and doing drugs –
because I tried to get away from him.
I entertained suicide to escape.

Whenever I hear *Midnight at the oasis...*
put your camel to bed... I embrace
that time: art scholarships, easy laughter,
lofty dreams of living in Chicago;
but I can't shake that badge of lies,
the raging guilt, the lack of trust
impressed upon me before
I could even reach my walk
with pomp and circumstance.

Unsettling Laughter

His laughter was always at my expense,
that sneering, demeaning laughter, always telling
others of my lack of talent at fixing his food
to his liking. He was hard to please and
always right, whether he was wrong or
just an asshole. He never laughed
when he yanked the ladle out of my hand
when I was stirring his food "incorrectly."
He never shared his ominous glares
with others at the dinner table
like he did with me: disgusted
because I didn't hold my fork properly –
after taking a bite of food, or repulsed
because I was the only person he knew
"who could make a marshmallow crunch"
due to my TMJ issue.
He didn't laugh when my jaw
needed medical attention
because he was saving to reupholster "his corvette;"
he was upset that he had to choose…
Funny, he never would let on to others
about the times he angrily pushed me down
on the bed or up against the wall, or
the way he'd form a fist and hit my folded knees
as I sat on the couch relaxing after fixing his lunch
for his thirty-minute break, how he'd laugh
at my pain as he left out the door – leaving for
work, leaving me wishing he'd leave for good.

Holding on to Me

I was young in 1981,
even though trapped
in a bad marriage,
with a man who
belittled and taunted
me about everything
I did from "not fixing
his food correctly," to
"laughing at the wrong
times," to "sleeping
too much," which became
his family's big joke…but

I had two daughters
whom I dearly loved, and
I had my music
that I listened to: "Don't Stop
Believing," and "Lady,"
that kept me dreaming
of better days ahead.
I had my art that I picked up
again, Ann's encouragement,
and other dear friends
who cheered me on
when I slipped into believing
the lies he said of me.

Dangerous Curves

While working at my uncle's restaurant
my crushes on waitresses
grabbed mother by the apron strings.
At fourteen I shouldn't have been collecting
8 x 10's of high school girls to hang
above my bed, youth as an obsession.

Did she call in the big guns
to kill me with kindness?
The kind a 27-year-old cop can give,
a dick full of promises,
and a spin behind the wheel
before turning legal –

in our driveway,
on country roads, day or night,
my head pushed down.
No one knows
what a contortionist I can be.
He laughed, "With your shoes off,
I could get slapped –
with statutory rape."

I ate his attention,
drank his direct lies.
At fifteen I was robbed.
My innocence was last seen
sipping cherry cokes with girlfriends
at the Chat and Chew.
Traveling with baggage
the size of Barry White,
I married at eighteen.
Bill, was twenty-three, safe,
and smitten with me.
Walking down the aisle,
my maid-of-honor's smile
was all I wanted to make
mine for a lifetime.

Eight years later, freedom
accelerated my taste for flirting.
Jack, Johnny, Bud and I rounded bars.
I two-stepped into many men's sheets,
quenching a lust for something sweeter
than singles mixers and wife beaters.
I found love between the mountains
of Tennessee – a satisfied Volunteer
for a long-distance romance
destined to last the long haul.
Five years of weekend bliss
spent in Polaroid positions
that would make Paris Hilton blush.
For miles we rolled until I found
 ex-wife was never legally divorced
from distanced Jim's charms.

Maybe I should've married Tony
in the middle of that road,
when he suggested
we'd make the best couple –
an arranged marriage for benefits.
He still could slip in with men, and I
could slip out
since Jim couldn't commit.

The road kept winding
through psycho paths,
empty lanes and lonesome tolls
until I shifted gears, met Maggie,
life passenger to share curves,
soft shoulders, and reflections
once deflected in my rearview mirror,
where ditched hitchhikers
echo closer than they appear.

The Day Truman Capote Died

The day Truman Capote died
my heart reeled from the headlines
that rivaled a non-fiction novel.
The story was: my friend
entered Head's Tavern
to purchase a 6-pack to go
when the six-foot-seven
ex-policeman slid his hand
between her legs to cop a feel,
hoping to poke a new notch in his belt.
When she pulled out of his clammy grip,
his cockiness shrunk.
Tempered by whiskey, and red-faced,
he picked her up as if she were a ragdoll,
hung her upside down by her ankles
and dropped her headfirst onto the floor
over and over and over again.
Gossip said she deserved the attack:
always teasing men with that smile and laughter,
and by daring to go into a tavern alone –
formerly called The Stag –
a place for manly men to gather,
tip back some booze and brag
about the latest doe
they bagged in cold blood.

The Last Time I Was Here

I remember this feeling
of ecstasy, of longing,
of belonging. Then when
I started falling deeper,
I found hard emotions from
my new partner throwing me
back into buried memories
of loving and being left,
being left when off guard,
of leaving and being
so far gone I felt I would
never come back
to try my luck
at romance again. Now
I am spinning out
of control, feeling lost
and familiar
all at once.

Her Perceptions

She only saw me
as an introvert,
the opposite of her
rigid, dominant
personality.
She chastised me
for laughing
at the end of sentences.

She found me annoying,
insecure, a pushover,
without knowing the real me –
a survivor
in life after being knocked
about literally and figuratively,

who finds a smile and laughter
as comfort. She didn't like
that I patted her, didn't
see it as affection, but as
a leftover maternal instinct
that she must endure.

When she belittled my life
as a teacher, poet,
artist, my not worshipping
money or her expensive wines,
I balked saying,
>*I am respected.*

She replied, staring and stiff:
>*I just don't see it.*

Alone in a Crowd

Here I am,
after moving to this new city, Toledo,
over four months ago,
and after making plans to hear
a poetry reading at the Toledo Museum
of Art, my best friend, stood me up – not even a call.
But, I ingest poems by Frank O'Hara,
everybody's friend, if they listen. Still.
Rosie the Riveter takes nothing
from nobody – I should learn that lesson.
And, I shouldn't have worried about my diet –
Oh! I could have fit in with Botero's subjects. Round
and around. A young boy exclaims "Whoa,
I thought that was a real person!"
as he jumps back from *The Executive,*
and I fade into the *Twelve Zodiac Figures
in Tang Dynasty Style.*
Funny, I don't feel like a monkey.
Let's be Frank –
Marisol was right,
I do feel "lonely in a crowded room" –
still waiting on that call.

Weddings

I never had
that wedding
other women
dream of:
the partner
of their dreams
appears in reality –

A wedding
day filled
with such joy
they felt
their heart
could burst
with rice
and confetti.

A wedding
where the future
is looked forward
to, knowing
they've made
the right choice.

A wedding
filled with truth –
walking down the aisle
to the one
truly loved.

More than
anything,
I wish
I could trade
in my three
weddings
for one
that meant
my heart
found
a home.

Relationships and Red Flags
(A Self-Help Poem)

Don't second guess yourself.
You've had so much experience
in this area, you could charge
good money for life lessons.
You see the writing on the wall

in other relationships.
You see it in your own.
You just give too many benefits
of doubt. Don't doubt
people aren't what they seem.

When someone says
they're going to do laundry
then come over afterward, and
it's been thirty years…they've
probably stood you up.

When you find yourself
struggling with a spouse
over a loaded gun –
they probably aren't long-term
marriage material.

When someone doesn't like
your sense of humor,
your pats of affection,
your being a teacher,
because of low income,
your friends,
your good-nature –
run.

Hopeful Relationships
(Love Still Tries to Crack My Lock)

In My New Apartment
for Maggie

If I would've died last night,
when the crack whore was down
the hall beating on a neighbor's door,
screaming "You punk ass bitch!
Open up! Let me in, Bob!" over and over,
and I didn't know if bullets would fly, and
I didn't know if she'd knock and pound her way here,
and I didn't know my cats could
pussyfoot so lightly in the middle of the night,
without a creaky croak from the hardwood floor,
I would've died happy, after
spending the evening with you, finding us
again, my head peacefully upon your breast,
listening to your heart thump, thump, thumping loud.

Surprise!

They say love happens
when you least expect it.

Being a hardcore skeptic
with many failed relationships
and a nearly four-year drought
of love or lust,
at fifty-six I resigned myself
to a life of celibacy, getting
my joy from cerebral adventures:
reading, writing, sharing my love
of poetry and teaching.

Lust was certainly left behind
in some dusty chamber of my mind,
and menopause dried up
memories that remained.

Then she came along, and
her smile got to me. I never anticipated
anything past one date. I knew
I could find enough excuses
not to have another, and when
we parted without a kiss,
it seemed so simple. I wouldn't
even have to say: *no thanks.*

But on my drive home
from Detroit, something happened –
I entertained thoughts of seeing her
again, of what kissing *her* might be like.
With no one around, I smiled.
When she texted
before I got home,
my cynical, hard-wired heart
sparked with life.

Rewriting Romance

It's like reading a good novel
energized by a surprise

twist – my heart flips through –
I feel the potential building,

my mind trips through
fragile pages; old love stories,

book-marked, long lived.
Dear diary told:

> *love*
> *no one*

locked tight so no one could

> pick.
> Click, click.

Unexpected images rush
back, keep me awake at night,

> color me
> less cynical –

a stranger. A new protagonist
coaxes me out of my own mystery.

In this pleasant summer air,

> the birds
> cheer me on,

urge me on. Chirp, chirp, tweet.
I'm showing signs - I'm not telling.

Those sweet texts linger in laughter.
I like the tease of a climax

as I turn tender within –
> opening up, fresh and
> full of possibilities.

My Heart Re-learns How to Ride

My once sheltered heart
is coasting –
it flutters at the sound
of your voice
as if cards playing in the spokes
shuffle faster and faster.
I'm convinced
to give in
without usual worry about:
    what if this, what if that, what if I fall….
I look into your brown eyes
deep and I'm taking off.

I try to peddle slow
with you
into this new territory:
an almost familiar touch,
a sexy smile.
I'm reminded
of the first time
learning to stay steady
without the safety
of rusty training wheels.

Then you call me
    honey or *darling*
and I feel like letting go
of the handle bars
trusting this
new
balance
will carry me
safely onward.

Paying the Price

I never forgot what a past
girlfriend said when I told her
I got a speeding ticket
going home from her place –
she said:

> *Silly, you're supposed*
> *to speed getting to me,*
> *not going away from me*

We both laughed, but
I didn't know how prophetic
those words would become.
Later, when at lesbian
U-Haul speed, I packed
my things, called my friends,
collected my cats, and
moved out after committing
a moving (in) violation,
then finding out we
were incompatible.

Twelve years later,
when I was sitting
off the side of Ormond Road,
Michigan blue lights
flashing in my rearview mirror.
I smiled at the implication.
I was traveling too fast
on my way to see Kathy –
maybe this ticket is worth
the price knowing that
speeding to see her
is a much better omen
than speeding away.

Unrequited Crush

She doesn't know
what warm feelings
she brings me –
when she's near
my heart thumps
as if it's keeping time
to Staying Alive
on a disco dance floor.

When she's not around
unannounced thoughts
of her sneak
into my mind, and alone
I smile as if I'm living
my dream, hoping
to star in her reality.

In a deep sleep
I dream; dreams
so vivid of her I believe
I'm conscious. In each,
she steals a kiss, or looks
at me with a promise
of a future I can taste.

Then, I wake to a world,
where she doesn't share
a same-sex love
interest in me, yet
just knowing she likes
me, somehow lessens
the blow of what
needs kept unknown.

Fragments
"I want things whole, but I love things broken"
                    -- Ellen Doré Watson

When I was young, I wanted the fairy tale ending,
the happily ever after – the two-people coming
together making a whole, but a deeper hole
is all I got each time I tried for my special story.
    There's the one about the police officer, 27, and
    me being 15 – thinking that his physical want
    was love. There's the one about the 23-year-old
    grease monkey and me at 16 – not wanting to be
    "unfaithful" to that cop, but it didn't matter
    what I wanted anyway. Was this love
    because he couldn't control himself with me?
Then there's the one about me marrying at 18,
to someone who I thought was safe –
only finding out that words, belittling, and keeping
me from family and friends hurt just as bad
as those who crossed physical boundaries, and then
another brief bad marriage, and then another
to someone who told me I would never tell him *"no"*
on our wedding night; he made good on that
promise and many others that I lived to regret –
until I escaped.
    Did I want these broken pieces
    my world kept scattering in? Every time I bounced back
    I thought I was whole, and would never make that
    mistake again. But there they were in different pieces
    than before: a married man who swore he wasn't –
    until it was too late. My first relationship with a woman
    when I came out – who was beginning her own journey
    to transgender. There's another woman that struggled
    with her own abuses, another with a long battle
    with addictions, and finally there was the narcissist
    who was a pro when it came to the art of gaslighting.
I gave them my best shot – each and every one
of them; I felt it was love…my storybook ending,
this time, had finally found me.
What I found in the end was cynicism,
then a long stint of being alone.
    Now I feel whole on my own – not wanting another person to
    furnish my fairy tale, to shatter my peace to pieces.

Lylanne Musselman

Photo by Alison Thompson

Lylanne Musselman, once a college dropout because of her fear of failing English Composition, found herself back in college 20 years later, fell in love with poetry and the writing process, and now teaches others to overcome their fear of writing. Since that breakthrough, her work has appeared in Pank, Flying Island, Ekphrastic Review, The New Verse News, Poetry Breakfast, and Rat's Ass Review, among others, and many anthologies, including Resurrection of a Sunflower, poems to honor Vincent van Gogh (Pski's Porch, 2017). A Pushcart Nominee twice, Musselman is the author of four poetry chapbooks, and co-author of a volume of poems. When she's not writing poetry, she writes plays (seven produced), and has found her second wind with her first love: visual art, exhibiting and winning awards in regional art shows. Musselman lives in her childhood home, taking care of her elderly mother and five much-loved cats.

It's Not Love, Unfortunately is a volume of poetry that explores experiences with relationships over a span of a lifetime; from finding out early on that moms and dads are not all like Ward and June Cleaver, to learning that boys are after more than friendship in junior high, to marrying at eighteen and learning what an abusive relationship is all about, to finding the survivor within, divorcing, and after years of searching for love...finally coming out around forty years old, the poet finds that relationships with women can be just as frustrating and abusive as those with men...and that no matter what station you are in life, and no matter what side of the fence you sit on...love never comes easy and is even harder to find. Nevertheless, this volume of poems will leave you with a few tears and a few smiles, but will never leave you feeling alone. No matter who you are, if you've ever loved or searched for love you will recognize yourself in these poems. If you're a Baby Boomer, you will find that the poet incorporates a lot of pop culture from the 1960s and 1970s that will bring memories rushing back, if you're a GenXer or a Millennial, you will find there's some familiar territory here for you too, but all readers will find the clear connection is relationships, for better or worse, make us into who we are. If we're lucky, we will have interesting stories (poems) to tell, even if "it's not love, unfortunately."

www.ingramcontent.com/pod-product-compliance
Lightning Source LLC
Chambersburg PA
CBHW081338080526
44588CB00017B/2665